TABLE OF CONTENT

Top 15 Test Taking Tips

1. Know the test directions, duration, topics, question types, how many questions
2. Setup a flexible study schedule at least 3-4 weeks before test day
3. Study during the time of day you are most alert, relaxed, and stress free
4. Maximize your learning style; visual learner use visual study aids, auditory learner use auditory study aids
5. Focus on your weakest knowledge base
6. Find a study partner to review with and help clarify questions
7. Practice, practice, practice
8. Get a good night's sleep; don't try to cram the night before the test
9. Eat a well balanced meal
10. Wear comfortable, loose fitting, layered clothing; prepare for it to be either cold or hot during the test
11. Eliminate the obviously wrong answer choices, then guess the first remaining choice
12. Pace yourself; don't rush, but keep working and move on if you get stuck
13. Maintain a positive attitude even if the test is going poorly
14. Keep your first answer unless you are positive it is wrong
15. Check your work, don't make a careless mistake

Lesson 1

Counting Maze

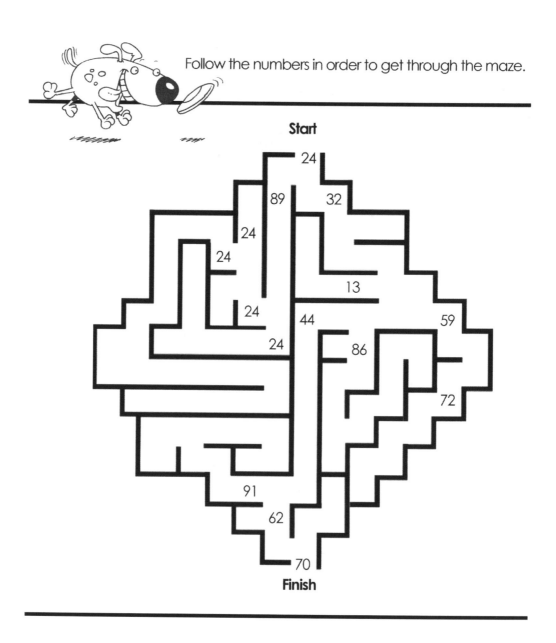

Follow the numbers in order to get through the maze.

Start

24

89   32

24

24

13

24

24   44   59

24   86

72

91

62

70

Finish

Lesson 2

Place Value

Draw an X over the third and twelfth spoons.

Draw an X over the fourth, ninth, and thirteenth boxes.

Draw an X over the eighth, tenth, and fourteenth lamps.

Draw an X over the first, eleventh, and fifteenth bags.

Draw an X over the second, fifth, and ninth objects.

Draw an X over the fourth, seventh, and thirteenth globes.

Lesson 3

Greater Than, Less Than or Equal - 2 Digit Numbers

Compare these 2 digit numbers and answer if each set is greater, less than or equal.

1. 22 $<$ 78

2. 91 ☐ 41

3. 47 ☐ 99

4. 65 ☐ 11

5. 99 ☐ 63

6. 71 ☐ 80

7. 39 ☐ 93

8. 10 ☐ 10

9. 17 ☐ 71

10. 49 ☐ 77

11. 83 ☐ 28

12. 22 ☐ 37

13. 13 ☐ 57

14. 93 ☐ 52

15. 22 ☐ 57

16. 22 ☐ 45

17. 22 ☐ 22

18. 78 ☐ 78

19. 42 ☐ 24

20. 31 ☐ 33

21. 63 ☐ 63

22. 88 ☐ 25

23. 74 ☐ 77

24. 22 ☐ 12

25. 32 ☐ 81

26. 98 ☐ 99

27. 75 ☐ 75

28. 22 ☐ 11

Lesson 4

Greater Than, Less Than or Equal - 3 Digit Numbers

Compare these 3 digit numbers and choose which is greater.

1. 399 < 789
2. 199 ☐ 108
3. 456 ☐ 156
4. 204 ☐ 151
5. 304 ☐ 301
6. 444 ☐ 458
7. 989 ☐ 745
8. 500 ☐ 501
9. 600 ☐ 789
10. 565 ☐ 564
11. 908 ☐ 656
12. 100 ☐ 102
13. 999 ☐ 998
14. 205 ☐ 789

15. 111 ☐ 108
16. 399 ☐ 871
17. 123 ☐ 654
18. 555 ☐ 178
19. 355 ☐ 878
20. 191 ☐ 109
21. 689 ☐ 489
22. 123 ☐ 124
23. 222 ☐ 229
24. 601 ☐ 502
25. 111 ☐ 211
26. 321 ☐ 320
27. 600 ☐ 789
28. 747 ☐ 789

Lesson 5

Rounding to the 10th

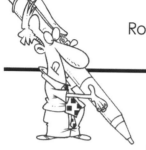

Round each number to the nearest 10th

1. 39 __40__

2. 18 _____

3. 89 _____

4. 22 _____

5. 27 _____

6. 56 _____

7. 78 _____

8. 11 _____

9. 69 _____

10. 72 _____

11. 29 _____

12. 81 _____

13. 99 _____

14. 76 _____

15. 14 _____

16. 95 _____

17. 77 _____

18. 13 _____

19. 58 _____

20. 21 _____

21. 63 _____

22. 34 _____

23. 84 _____

24. 90 _____

25. 17 _____

26. 84 _____

27. 72 _____

28. 19 _____

Lesson 6

Rounding to the nearest 100

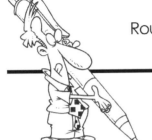

Round each number to the nearest 100th

1. 399 __400__

2. 452 _____

3. 124 _____

4. 695 _____

5. 230 _____

6. 425 _____

7. 475 _____

8. 205 _____

9. 244 _____

10. 111 _____

11. 587 _____

12. 299 _____

13. 199 _____

14. 787 _____

15. 754 _____

16. 329 _____

17. 285 _____

18. 205 _____

19. 912 _____

20. 879 _____

21. 325 _____

22. 132 _____

23. 897 _____

24. 289 _____

25. 475 _____

26. 441 _____

27. 654 _____

28. 321 _____

Lesson 7

Count Forward by 100's

Count forward by 100's

100		300			600		800

Count forward by 100's

	399	499		699			

Count forward by 100's

42							742

Count forward by 100's

289		489			789		

Count forward by 100's

	102		302				

Lesson 8

Arrange Numbers from Smallest to Largest

Arrange the numbers in order from smallest to largest.

1. 188	_2_	**2.** 879	___	**3.** 200	___
13	_1_	233	___	756	___
689	_4_	54	___	89	___
346	_3_	955	___	2	___

4. 346	___	**5.** 421	___	**6.** 358	___
745	___	465	___	101	___
989	___	777	___	7	___
124	___	758	___	45	___

7. 125	___	**8.** 10	___	**9.** 422	___
785	___	2	___	420	___
658	___	787	___	358	___
9	___	512	___	785	___

- 13 -

Lesson 9

Arrange Numbers from Largest to Smallest

Arrange the numbers in order from largest to smallest .

1. 123	_4_	**2.** 564	___	**3.** 54	___
676	_2_	2	___	123	___
879	_1_	99	___	124	___
333	_3_	612	___	53	___

4. 202	___	**5.** 99	___	**6.** 125	___
457	___	45	___	141	___
589	___	54	___	223	___
2	___	470	___	789	___

7. 727	___	**8.** 123	___	**9.** 623	___
252	___	233	___	1	___
412	___	451	___	999	___
786	___	356	___	2	___

Lesson 10

Understanding Place Value 1

The place value of a digit is shown by where it is in the number. Add the tens and ones to get your total.

1. 4 Tens + 9 Ones = 49

2. 2 Tens + 0 Ones =

3. 6 Tens + 5 Ones =

4. 5 Tens + 5 Ones =

5. 9 Tens + 1 Ones =

6. 3 Tens + 7 Ones =

7. 4 Tens + 2 Ones =

8. 7 Tens + 5 Ones =

9. 3 Tens + 9 Ones =

10. 6 Tens + 7 Ones =

11. 1 Tens + 3 Ones =

12. 8 Tens + 9 Ones =

13. 5 Tens + 8 Ones =

Understanding Place Value 2

Help Barry the bear solve these problems.

1. $600 + 90 + 5 = 695$

2. $100 + 70 + 3 =$

3. $400 + 60 + 1 =$

4. $200 + 20 + 9 =$

5. $900 + 30 + 4 =$

6. $300 + 10 + 8 =$

7. $800 + 80 + 8 =$

8. $500 + 70 + 1 =$

9. $900 + 90 + 9 =$

10. $400 + 10 + 5 =$

11. $300 + 70 + 9 =$

12. $100 + 70 + 4 =$

13. $500 + 20 + 1 =$

14. $800 + 10 + 3 =$

15. $700 + 10 + 9 =$

16. $500 + 60 + 1 =$

17. $600 + 80 + 3 =$

18. $400 + 90 + 7 =$

19. $100 + 20 + 3 =$

20. $700 + 30 + 1 =$

21. $200 + 50 + 7 =$

22. $800 + 20 + 2 =$

23. $100 + 90 + 7 =$

24. $400 + 50 + 5 =$

25. $600 + 90 + 5 =$

26. $700 + 10 + 9 =$

27. $300 + 70 + 1 =$

28. $100 + 20 + 0 =$

Understanding Place Value 3

 Help Russell the alligator solve these problems.

1.   7 Hundreds   +   4 Tens   +   9 Ones   =   749

2.   4 Hundreds   +   2 Tens   +   0 Ones   =

3.   5 Hundreds   +   1 Tens   +   5 Ones   =

4.   1 Hundred   +   5 Tens   +   5 Ones   =

5.   3 Hundreds   +   9 Tens   +   1 Ones   =

6.   8 Hundreds   +   3 Tens   +   7 Ones   =

7.   4 Hundreds   +   4 Tens   +   2 Ones   =

8.   9 Hundreds   +   7 Tens   +   5 Ones   =

9.   6 Hundreds   +   2 Tens   +   0 Ones   =

10. 2 Hundreds   +   6 Tens   +   7 Ones   =

11. 4 Hundreds   +   0 Tens   +   3 Ones   =

12. 3 Hundreds   +   8 Tens   +   9 Ones   =

13. 2 Hundreds   +   3 Tens   +   8 Ones   =

14. 8 Hundreds   +   5 Tens   +   6 Ones   =

15. 4 Hundreds   +   1 Tens   +   4 Ones   =

Lesson 11

Writing Out Place Value 1

Write out each number.

1. 76   Seventy-Six
2. 34   _____
3. 59   _____
4. 13   _____
5. 99   _____
6. 85   _____
7. 24   _____
8. 42   _____
9. 23   _____
10. 64   _____
11. 59   _____
12. 29   _____
13. 95   _____
14. 67   _____
15. 49   _____

Writing Out Place Value 2

Write out each number.

1. 249   Two Hundred Forty-Nine
2. 767   _____
3. 653   _____
4. 111   _____
5. 248   _____
6. 129   _____
7. 890   _____
8. 435   _____
9. 211   _____
10. 147   _____
11. 654   _____
12. 174   _____
13. 697   _____
14. 387   _____
15. 311   _____

Lesson 12

Recognizing Patterns 1

 Follow the directions in each section.

Write the numbers or letters that are next in order.

1. 1, __, 3, A, 4, 5, 6, __,   **2.** 4, 3, __, 1, D, C, __, A,

3. A, B, __, D, E, __, G, H,   **4.** 1, A, 2, B, __, C, 4, __,

---

Write the number that is one less.

1. __, 8   **2.** __, 4   **3.** __,10 **4.** __,22 **5.** __, 78

6. __, 16   **7.** __,19   **8.** __,47 **9.** __,33 **10.** __,96

11. __,51   **12.** __,74   **13.** __, 6 **14.** __,11 **15.** __,14

Write the number that is one greater.

1. __,12   **2.** __, 8   **3.** __,17 **4.** __,52 **5.** __, 3

6. __,77   **7.** __,41   **8.** __,63 **9.** __, 4 **10.** __,15

11. __,36   **12.** __,25   **13.** __,12 **14.** __, 8 **15.** __,19

Lesson 13

Recognizing Patterns 2 - Using a Number Chart

 Using the chart below, answer each question.

1	2	3	4	5	6	7	8	9	10
11	12	13	14	15	16	17	18	19	20
21	22	23	24	25	26	27	28	29	30
31	32	33	34	35	36	37	38	39	40
41	42	43	44	45	46	47	48	49	50
51	52	53	54	55	56	57	58	59	60
61	62	63	64	65	66	67	68	69	70
71	72	73	74	75	76	77	78	79	80
81	82	83	84	85	86	87	88	89	90
91	92	93	94	95	96	97	98	99	100

1. Finish the pattern starting with 1,11,21

   31, 41, 51, 61, 71, 81, 91

2. Finish the pattern starting with 7,17,27

3. Finish the pattern starting with 1,12,23

4. Finish the pattern starting with 10,20,30

Lesson 14

Recognizing Patterns 3 - Fill in the Number Chart

 Fill in the missing numbers using 10s.

10	20		40			70		90	
110		130		150	160		180		
210			240		260			290	300
310	320			350			380		400
	420	430	440				480		
510		530		550	560		580		600
	620	630			660	670		690	
710			740	750					800
	820		840		860	870		890	
		930	940	950					1000

Lesson 1

Single-Column Addition

Add the numbers, then circle the sum
that is bigger in each set.

1. 7   3
  + 2   + 5
   ⑨   8

2. 5   2
  + 4   + 1

3. 5   3
  + 5   + 1

4. 1   8
  + 2   + 3

5. 5   9
  + 2   + 5

6. 6   7
  + 1   + 4

7. 2   4
  + 0   + 7

8. 3   8
  + 2   + 5

9. 1   9
  + 8   + 5

10. 2   6
   + 7   + 6

11. 8   4
   + 9   + 8

Lesson 2

Single-Column Addition - Greater Than, Less Than or Equal

 Add the numbers, then decide if the first sum is greater than, less than or equal to the second.

1. 2   3
    + 2   + 9
    ‾‾‾   ‾‾‾
      4   $<$ 12

2. 8   2
    + 1   + 7
    ‾‾‾   ‾‾‾
      ☐

3. 4   6
    + 8   + 5
    ‾‾‾   ‾‾‾
      ☐

4. 5   3
    + 2   + 6
    ‾‾‾   ‾‾‾
      ☐

5. 1   1
    + 9   + 6
    ‾‾‾   ‾‾‾
      ☐

6. 5   6
    + 8   + 5
    ‾‾‾   ‾‾‾
      ☐

7. 8   1
    + 1   + 1
    ‾‾‾   ‾‾‾
      ☐

8. 7   4
    + 2   + 5
    ‾‾‾   ‾‾‾
      ☐

9. 8   7
    + 8   + 2
    ‾‾‾   ‾‾‾
      ☐

10. 1   3
     + 2   + 3
     ‾‾‾   ‾‾‾
       ☐

11. 5   7
     + 7   + 7
     ‾‾‾   ‾‾‾
       ☐

Lesson 3

Single-Column Addition - Math Race

Add the numbers. Circle each answer on the
racetrack as you go and see who wins the race.

**Finish
Line**

9	3	1	5	8
2	6	4	7	10

1. 1
+ 1
___
2

2. 2
+ 7
___

3. 2
+ 1
___

4. 4
+ 2
___

5. 1
+ 0
___

6. 2
+ 2
___

7. 2
+ 3
___

8. 3
+ 4
___

9. 6
+ 2
___

10. 7
+ 3
___

Lesson 4

2-Digit Addition - Regrouping

How to regroup: When the numbers in the ones column add up to a number larger than 10, the first digit of that number carries over to the tens column.

Tens	Ones
1	6
+	5
	11

Tens	Ones
1	
1	6
+	5
	1

Tens	Ones
1	
1	6
+	5
2	1

Solve the problems below.

1. 1 6	**2.** 3 8	**3.** 7 2	**4.** 5 6	**5.** 4 9	**6.** 2 6
+ 5	+ 2	+ 9	+ 6	+ 6	+ 5
2 1					

7. 3 7	**8.** 6 9	**9.** 2 8	**10.** 2 4	**11.** 9 4	**12.** 7 7
+ 4	+ 5	+ 7	+ 9	+ 8	+ 6

Lesson 5

2-Digit Addition - Number Find

Solve the problems below, then circle the answers hidden in the scene.

$$
\begin{array}{r} 41 \\ + \ 8 \\ \hline 49 \end{array}
\qquad
\begin{array}{r} 64 \\ + \ 4 \\ \hline \end{array}
\qquad
\begin{array}{r} 92 \\ + \ 7 \\ \hline \end{array}
\qquad
\begin{array}{r} 45 \\ + \ 5 \\ \hline \end{array}
\qquad
\begin{array}{r} 24 \\ + \ 3 \\ \hline \end{array}
\qquad
\begin{array}{r} 37 \\ + \ 2 \\ \hline \end{array}
$$

$$
\begin{array}{r} 16 \\ + \ 1 \\ \hline \end{array}
\qquad
\begin{array}{r} 26 \\ + \ 9 \\ \hline \end{array}
\qquad
\begin{array}{r} 57 \\ + \ 7 \\ \hline \end{array}
\qquad
\begin{array}{r} 19 \\ + \ 4 \\ \hline \end{array}
\qquad
\begin{array}{r} 21 \\ + \ 7 \\ \hline \end{array}
\qquad
\begin{array}{r} 85 \\ + \ 9 \\ \hline \end{array}
$$

Lesson 6

Commutative Property 1

Commutative property means that even if the order of numbers is changed in an addition problem, the sum will always be the same.

Complete the problems by writing the missing numbers.

1. <u>90</u> + 5 = 95   **2.** ___ + 6 = 77

    90 + <u>5</u> = 95   71 + ___ = 77

3. ___ + 70 = 80   **4.** ___ + 7 = 15

    10 + ___ = 80   8 + ___ = 15

4. ___ + 25 = 46   **5.** ___ + 74 = 98

    21 + ___ = 46   24 + ___ = 98

6. ___ + 13 = 20   **7.** ___ + 13 = 64

    7 + ___ = 20   51 + ___ = 64

8. ___ + 87 = 92   **9.** ___ + 20 = 29

    5 + ___ = 92   9 + ___ = 29

10. ___ + 3 = 65   **11.** ___ + 3 = 34

    62 + ___ = 65   31 + ___ = 34

Commutative Property 2

Commutative property means that even if the order of numbers is changed in an addition problem, the sum will always be the same.

Complete the problems by writing the missing numbers.

1. 11   11
     + 5   + 5
     ———   ———
      16   16

2. 4   __
     + __   + 3
     ———   ———
      7   7

3. 45   __
     + __   + 9
     ———   ———
      54   54

4. 2   __
     + __   + 7
     ———   ———
      9   9

5. 27   __
     + __   + 1
     ———   ———
      28   28

6. 39   __
     + __   + 2
     ———   ———
      41   41

7. 22   __
     + __   + 5
     ———   ———
      27   27

8. 71   __
     + __   + 8
     ———   ———
      79   79

9. 9   __
     + __   + 1
     ———   ———
      10   10

10. 7   __
      + __   + 3
      ———   ———
       10   10

11. 56   __
      + __   + 5
      ———   ———
       61   61

12. 62   __
      + __   + 6
      ———   ———
       68   68

Lesson 7

2-Digit Addition 1

To do two digit addition, we first add the numbers in the ones column, then we add the numbers in the tens column.

First the ones

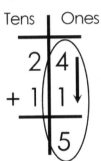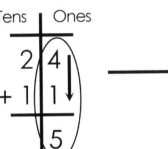

Then the tens

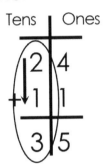

Solve the problems below.

1. 2 4
    + 1 1
    -----
    3 5

2. 7 3
    + 2 3
    -----

3. 2 4
    + 1 5
    -----

4. 6 4
    + 2 0
    -----

5. 4 8
    + 5 1
    -----

6. 5 3
    + 3 2
    -----

7. 6 3
    + 2 1
    -----

8. 1 5
    + 1 0
    -----

9. 5 6
    + 3 2
    -----

10. 4 9
    + 4 0
    -----

11. 3 8
    + 6 1
    -----

12. 7 8
    + 2 1

2-Digit Addition 2

 To do two digit addition, we first add the numbers in the ones column, then we add the numbers in the tens column.

Solve the problems below.

1. 64
    +35

    99

2. 28
    +57

3. 77
    +39

4. 12
    +34

5. 78
    +29

6. 13
    +64

7. 48
    +73

8. 80
    +26

9. 78
    +21

10. 45
    +51

11. 68
    +28

12. 72
    +23

13. 39
    +27

14. 60
    +85

15. 15
    +70

16. 28
    +23

17. 45
    +56

18. 16
    +30

Lesson 8

3-Digit Single-Column Addition 1

Adding three or more numbers is just like adding two.
Always remember to count them out.

```
   4
   5
 + 3
 ────
  12
```

1. 5
4
+ 7

2. 1
1
+ 5

3. 9
4
+ 6

4. 2
2
+ 7

5. 6
1
+ 8

6. 4
7
+ 1

7. 5
4
+ 7

8. 6
2
+ 9

9. 2
1
+ 1

10. 7
8
+ 8

11. 5
4
+ 7

12. 6
2
+ 3

13. 1
8
+ 9

3-Digit Single-Column Addition 2

Adding three or more numbers is just like adding two.
Always remember to count them out.

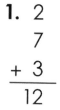

1. 2
   7
   + 3
   ___
   12

2. 1
   7
   + 2
   ___

3. 2
   8
   + 4
   ___

4. 6
   3
   + 3
   ___

5. 9
   4
   + 8
   ___

6. 2
   5
   + 1
   ___

7. 7
   0
   + 5
   ___

8. 3
   2
   + 9
   ___

9. 5
   4
   + 1
   ___

10. 3
    2
    + 9
    ___

11. 7
    9
    + 0
    ___

12. 5
    5
    + 4
    ___

13. 3
    2
    + 3
    ___

14. 6
    4
    + 9
    ___

Lesson 9

4-Digit Single-Column Addition 1

Adding four or more numbers is a lot like adding two or three. Always remember to add them in sets.

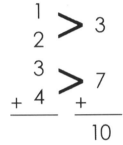

```
  1              6
   > 3           > 9
  2              3
  3              4
   > 7           > 9
+ 4    +       + 5    +
  ─────          ─────
   10             18
```

1. 4
       5
       3
    + 1
    ─────

2. 8
       1
       2
    + 1
    ─────

3. 5
       3
       3
    + 9
    ─────

4. 1
       2
       2
    + 7
    ─────

5. 7
       4
       2
    + 6
    ─────

6. 5
       6
       6
    + 1
    ─────

- 35 -

4-Digit Single-Column Addition 2

Adding four or more numbers is a lot like adding two
or three. Always remember to add them in sets.

1. 1
    5
    3
  + 9

2. 5
    9
    7
  + 2

3. 6
    0
    4
  + 7

4. 3
    2
    9
  + 4

5. 4
    4
    5
  + 5

6. 7
    4
    2
  + 1

7. 9
    9
    2
  + 3

8. 7
    3
    3
  + 7

9. 1
    5
    1
  + 1

10. 5
     5
     5
   + 9

11. 2
     7
     2
   + 9

Lesson 10

Number Table Addition

Use the addition table to fill in the blanks.

+	1	2	3	4	5	6	7	8	9
1		3							
2				6					11
3	4								
4		6							
5						11			
6									
7			10						
8	9							16	
9				13					

Lesson 1

Subtraction: Removing Objects

Cross out the number of items in the first box.
In the second box, write the number of items left.

| 3 | | 4 |

| 6 | | |

| 4 | | |

| 9 | | |

| 11 | | |

Lesson 2

Single-Column Subtraction

Subtract the numbers, then circle the number that is smaller in each set.

1. 7   5
  - 5 - 4
   2   ①

2. 6   5
  - 4 - 1

3. 3   9
  - 2 - 7

4. 4   5
  - 1 - 1

5. 9   8
  - 2 - 5

6. 2   5
  - 1 - 2

7. 8   6
  - 3 - 5

8. 6   9
  - 4 - 5

9. 7   8
  - 2 - 1

10. 2   3
   - 2 - 2

11. 4   3
   - 3 - 1

Single-Column Subtraction - Greater Than, Less Than or Equal

Solve both equations in each set using subtraction. Then decide if the first difference in each set is greater than, less than, or equal to the second.

1. 6   9
    - 2   - 4
    ───── ─────
     4 |<| 5

2. 7   3
    - 2   - 1
    ───── ─────
       □

3. 2   8
    - 2   - 5
    ───── ─────
       □

4. 3   5
    - 1   - 4
    ───── ─────
       □

5. 8   2
    - 7   - 1
    ───── ─────
       □

6. 10   5
    - 2   - 3
    ───── ─────
       □

7. 3   9
    - 1   - 2
    ───── ─────
       □

8. 6   8
    - 5   - 1
    ───── ─────
       □

9. 2   3
    - 2   - 1
    ───── ─────
       □

10. 6   8
    - 1   - 5
    ───── ─────
       □

11. 10   5
    - 7   - 2
    ───── ─────
       □

Lesson 3

Single-Column Subtraction - Math Race

Subtract the numbers. Circle each answer on the racetrack as you go and see who wins the race.

5	1	2	7	9	**Finish Line**
2	8	3	4	6	

1. 7
  - 2
  ___
  5

2. 5
  - 3
  ___

3. 9
  - 1
  ___

4. 4
  - 3
  ___

5. 6
  - 3
  ___

6. 10
  - 8
  ___

7. 9
  - 5
  ___

8. 8
  - 1
  ___

9. 9
  - 3
  ___

10. 10
  - 1
  ___

Lesson 4

2-Digit Subtraction 1

 **In subtraction** - When the top digit has two numbers and the bottom digit has one, the digit in the tens column just drops down into the total.

First the ones	Then the tens

First the ones

Tens | Ones

3 8
−   4
‑‑‑‑‑
    4

Then the tens

Tens | Ones

3 8
−   4
‑‑‑‑‑
3   4

Solve the problems below.

1. 7 5   2. 3 9   3. 5 6   4. 1 2   5. 2 3   6. 1 7
   - 2   - 7   - 5   - 1   - 3   - 5
   ‑‑‑‑   ‑‑‑‑   ‑‑‑‑   ‑‑‑‑   ‑‑‑‑   ‑‑‑‑
   7 3

7. 2 9   8. 4 7   9. 8 6   10. 6 5   11. 8 8   12. 4 4
   - 5   - 1   - 6   - 1   - 5   - 2
   ‑‑‑‑   ‑‑‑‑   ‑‑‑‑   ‑‑‑‑   ‑‑‑‑   ‑‑‑‑

Lesson 5

2-Digit Subtraction 2

 When doing two digit subtraction, subtract from the ones column first, then the tens column.

1. 5 5
   - 1
   —————
   5 4

2. 2 7
   - 7

3. 1 4
   - 2

4. 3 9
   - 5

5. 4 2
   - 1

6. 8 5
   - 3

7. 3 2
   - 1

8. 4 8
   - 4

9. 1 9
   - 7

10. 3 7
   - 6

11. 9 6
   - 5

12. 5 4
   - 4

13. 2 5
   - 3

14. 3 7
   - 6

15. 1 9
   - 5

16. 7 5
   - 4

17. 3 6
   - 5

18. 2 2
   - 1

19. 4 9
   - 7

20. 7 1
   - 1

21. 5 4
   - 3

22. 2 9
   - 6

23. 1 8
   - 4

Lesson 6

2-Digit Subtraction - Number Find

Solve the problems below, then circle the answers hidden in the scene.

41 - 1 --- 40	11 - 2	16 - 9	89 - 3	21 - 3	3 - 1
23 - 10	77 - 5	12 - 6	61 - 1	39 - 9	18 - 6

Lesson 7

2-Digit Subtraction 3

When doing two digit subtraction, subtract from the ones column first, then the tens column.

First the ones

Tens | Ones

```
  3 6
- 1 2
    4
```

Then the tens

Tens | Ones

```
  3 6
- 1 2
  2 4
```

Solve the problems below.

1. 2 4   **2.** 3 9   **3.** 7 9   **4.** 4 2   **5.** 6 8   **6.** 1 7
  - 1 2   - 2 7   - 5 5   - 3 1   - 4 3   - 1 5
    1 2

7. 5 9   **8.** 9 7   **9.** 2 6   **10.** 3 9   **11.** 2 8   **12.** 6 4
  - 3 5   - 1 1   - 1 6   - 2 1   - 2 5   - 4 2

- 46 -

2-Digit Subtraction 4

When doing two digit subtraction, subtract from the ones
column first, then the tens column.

1. 24
−11
‾‾‾
13

2. 39
−27

3. 84
−62

4. 76
−55

5. 32
−10

6. 94
−50

7. 17
−15

8. 27
−14

9. 35
−21

10. 67
−46

11. 15
−10

12. 59
−41

13. 27
−16

14. 44
−40

15. 38
−21

16. 76
−24

17. 16
−15

18. 72
−31

19. 49
−27

20. 54
−23

21. 75
−51

22. 29
−21

23. 72
−51

Lesson 8

2-Digit Subtraction - Borrowing 1

 When doing two digit subtraction, subtract from the ones column first, then the tens column.

If the top number in the ones column is larger than the bottom, you have to borrow from the tens column.

Tens	Ones
4	2
- 1	5

Tens	Ones
3	12
4̸	2̸
- 1	5

Tens	Ones
3	12
4̸	2̸ ↓
- 1	5 ↓
	7

Tens	Ones
3	12
↓ 4̸	2̸
- ↓1	5
2	7

Solve the problems

1.	6 1	2.	5 4	3.	8 4	4.	9 1	5.	2 0	6.	6 8
	- 2 4		- 1 9		- 4 6		- 7 3		- 1 1		- 4 7
	3 7										

7.	2 4	8.	1 8	9.	3 3	10.	5 5	11.	7 4	12.	9 2
	- 1 9		- 9		- 2 1		- 4 9		- 5 5		- 3 9

2-Digit Subtraction - Borrowing 2

When doing two digit subtraction, subtract from the ones column first, then the tens column.

If the top number in the ones column is smaller than the bottom, you have to borrow from the tens column.

Solve the problems

1. 71
  - 28

    43

2. 57
  - 18

3. 44
  - 36

4. 34
  - 19

5. 70
  - 16

6. 78
  - 42

7. 21
  - 15

8. 74
  - 8

9. 73
  - 28

10. 93
   - 47

11. 64
   - 53

12. 62
   - 38

13. 31
   - 12

14. 79
   - 43

15. 91
   - 89

16. 67
   - 18

17. 21
   - 13

18. 35
   - 17

19. 71
   - 62

20. 32
   - 27

21. 92
   - 51

22. 73
   - 41

23. 73
   - 14

24. 91
   - 84

Lesson 9

Writing out 2-Digit Subtraction Problems 1

Write out these subtraction problems in columns and work them out.

1. 28 - 12

```
  2 8
- 1 2
─────
  1 6
─────
```

2. 65 - 37

```
-
─────

─────
```

3. 69 - 51

```
-
─────

─────
```

4. 12 - 10

```
-
─────

─────
```

5. 85 - 72

```
-
─────

─────
```

6. 51 - 43

```
-
─────

─────
```

7. 30 - 27

```
-
─────

─────
```

8. 96 - 53

```
-
─────

─────
```

Writing out 2-Digit Subtraction Problems 2

 Write out these subtraction problems in columns and work them out.

1. 95 - 44

\-
_____

_____

2. 59 - 15

\-
_____

_____

3. 62 - 32

\-
_____

_____

4. 47 - 29

\-
_____

_____

5. 58 - 41

\-
_____

_____

6. 70 - 39

\-
_____

_____

7. 99 - 22

\-
_____

_____

8. 30 - 19

\-
_____

_____

Lesson 10

Subtraction Word Problems

Use subtraction to solve.

1. George has three dogs. Sally has one dog. How many more dogs does George have than Sally? _____

2. Emma had nine pieces of candy. She ate three. How many pieces of candy does she have left? _____

3. David needs to run six miles to finish the race. He has run two so far. How many miles does he have left to run? _____

4. The school day is seven hours. Mark has been at school for four hours. How many hours does he have left? _____

5. Jimmy's dog weighed 80 pounds. He lost 17 pounds. How much does he weigh now? _____

Fractions are the numbers that make up part of a whole.

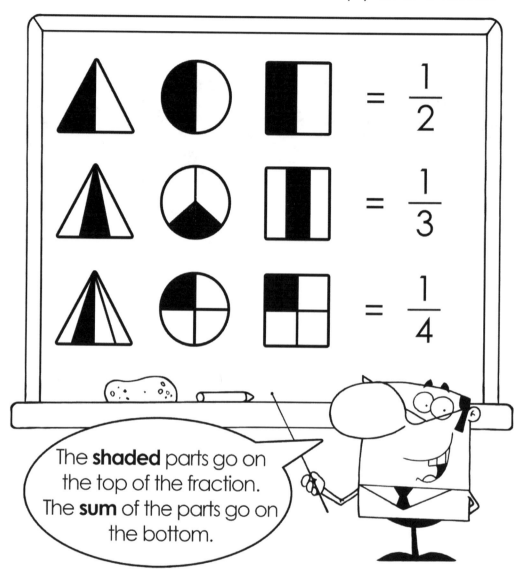

The **shaded** parts go on the top of the fraction. The **sum** of the parts go on the bottom.

Lesson 1

Halving

Shade in half of each shape below.

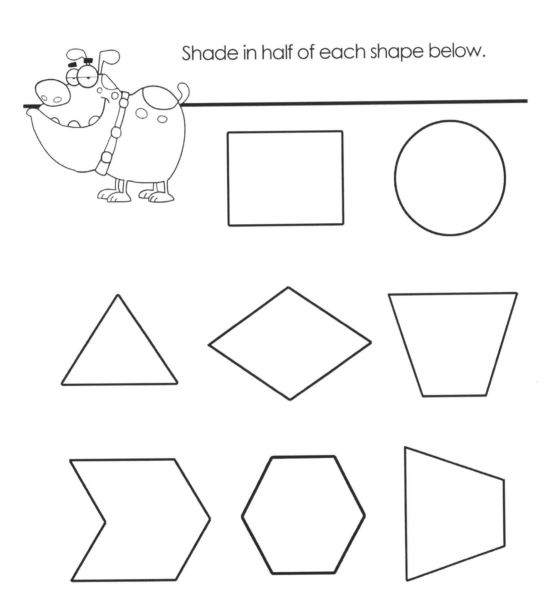

Lesson 2

Identifying Fractions 1

Color the shapes to match the fractions.

$\frac{1}{2}$ = ◭	$\frac{1}{3}$ = ◯
$\frac{1}{4}$ = ◯	$\frac{1}{2}$ = ▢
$\frac{1}{3}$ = ▢	$\frac{1}{3}$ = △
$\frac{1}{2}$ = ◯	$\frac{1}{4}$ = ▢

Lesson 3

Identifying Fractions 2

Color the shapes to match the fractions.

$\dfrac{1}{3}$ =

$\dfrac{2}{6}$ =

$\dfrac{1}{4}$ =

$\dfrac{5}{6}$ =

$\dfrac{2}{3}$ =

$\dfrac{7}{9}$ =

$\dfrac{3}{8}$ =

$\dfrac{1}{2}$ =

Lesson 4

Writing Fractions 1

 Write the fractions in number form. The shaded part goes on top of the fraction.

 = $\frac{1}{2}$ =

 =   =

 =   =

 =   =

Writing Fractions 2

Write out the fractions in words. Write the shaded part as the first word.

_____

one third   _____

_____   _____

_____   _____

_____   _____

Lesson 5

Identifying Fractions 3

Color in the faces to match the fractions.

$\dfrac{1}{4}$ =

$\dfrac{7}{8}$ =

$\dfrac{8}{11}$ =

$\dfrac{2}{5}$ =

$\dfrac{1}{3}$ =

$\dfrac{1}{2}$ =

Lesson 6

Writing Fractions 3

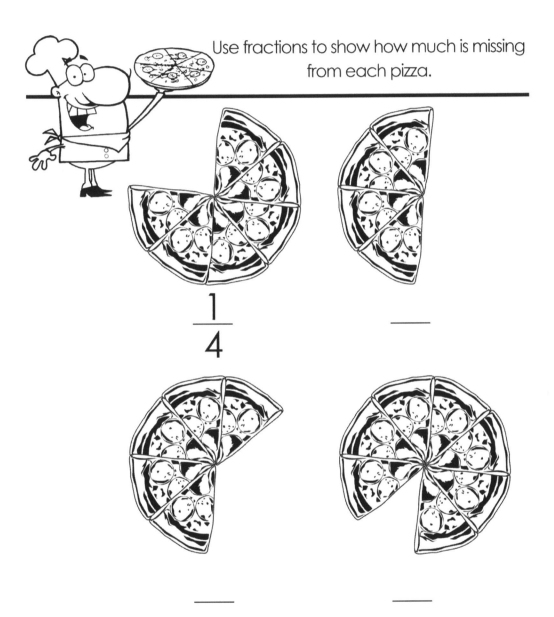

Use fractions to show how much is missing from each pizza.

$\frac{1}{4}$

_____

_____   _____

Lesson 7

Fraction Word Problems

Solve these fraction problems by coloring in the correct area.

1. Jimmy ate half of his sandwich. Color half of his sandwich.

2. Amy can have one third of this cupcake. Color one third of her cupcake.

3. Penny ate one quarter of the pizza. Color one quarter of her pizza.

Lesson 8

Graphing 1

Count the hamburgers in each row.
Color the boxes to match the numbers

Graphing 2

Count the tomatoes in each row.
Color the boxes to match the numbers

Lesson 9

Graphing 3 - Identifying Coordinates

To find places on a graph, start at 0, count across, then up. These are called coordinates.

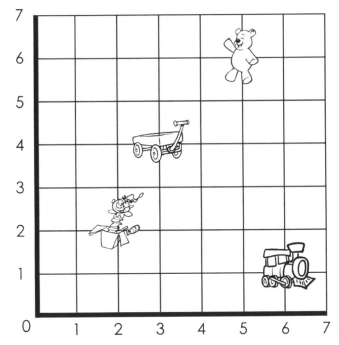

Write the coordinates for each toy in the blanks.

Across   Up   Across   Up   Across   Up   Across   Up

_3_ , _4_   ___ , ___   ___ , ___   ___ , ___

Graphing 4 - Identifying Coordinates

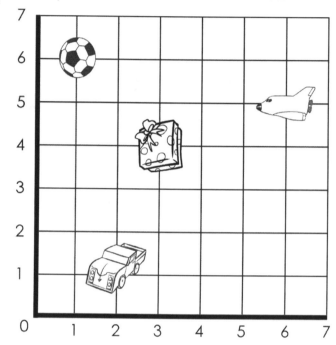

To find places on a graph, start at 0, count across, then up. These are called coordinates.

Write the coordinates for each object in the blanks.

Across	Up	Across	Up	Across	Up	Across	Up
1	6	___	___	___	___	___	___

Lesson 10

Graphing Word Problems

Use the graph to answer the questions.

Lily	🍭 🍭 🍭 🍭 🍭 🍭 🍭 🍭
Dave	🍭 🍭 🍭 🍭 🍭 🍭
Sally	🍭 🍭 🍭 🍭 🍭 🍭 🍭 🍭 🍭
Tim	🍭 🍭 🍭 🍭 🍭

1. Lily has how many more pieces than Tim? _____

2. _____ has the most candy.

3. _____ has the least amount of candy.

4. Sally has how many more pieces of candy than Tim? _____

5. Write each kid's name and how many pieces of candy they have.

_____

Money: Coins

Each coin has its own value.

= 1 penny = 1¢

= 1 nickel = 5¢

= 1 dime = 10¢

= 1 quarter = 25¢

We add the coins together to get the values.

Money: Bills

Each bill has its own value.

 = One Dollar

= $1

 = Five Dollars

= $5

 = Ten Dollars

= $10

 = Twenty Dollars

= $20

We add the bills together to get the values.

Lesson 1

Counting Change 1

Write how many of the missing coin you need to buy each object.

	(quarter)	(dime)	(nickel)	(penny)
38¢	1	1		3
68¢	2	1	1	
87¢	2		1	2

Counting Change 2

Write how many of the missing coin you need to buy each object.

	Quarter	Dime	Nickel	Penny
Iron 59¢	2	0	1	
Tree 42¢	1	1		2
Telephone 67¢		1	1	2

Counting Change 3

Circle or color how many coins you need to buy each item.

Lesson 2

Making Change 1

How much change do you get back for each object?

Price	You Pay	Work out problem	Change
3¢ (light bulb)	nickel	$\begin{array}{r} 5 \\ -\ 3 \\ \hline \end{array}$	2 ¢
18¢ (sandwich)	quarter		____ ¢
4¢ (banana)	dime		____ ¢
12¢ (spoon)	quarter		____ ¢

Making Change 2

How much change do you get back for each object?

Price	You Pay	Work out problem	Change
38¢		$\begin{array}{r} 50 \\ -\ 38 \\ \hline \end{array}$	12 ¢
62¢			_____ ¢
57¢			_____ ¢
81¢			_____ ¢

Lesson 3

Cents and Dollars

 Write in each box how many pieces of change you need to equal each bill.

How many =  $\boxed{4}$

How many =

How many =

How many =

Lesson 4

Dollars and Larger Bills

 Write in each box how many pieces of change you need to equal each bill.

How many  =  5

How many  =

How many  =

How many  =

Lesson 5

Dollars - Greater Than, Less Than or Equal

Compare the money groups. Write in the box which group is greater than, less than, or equal.

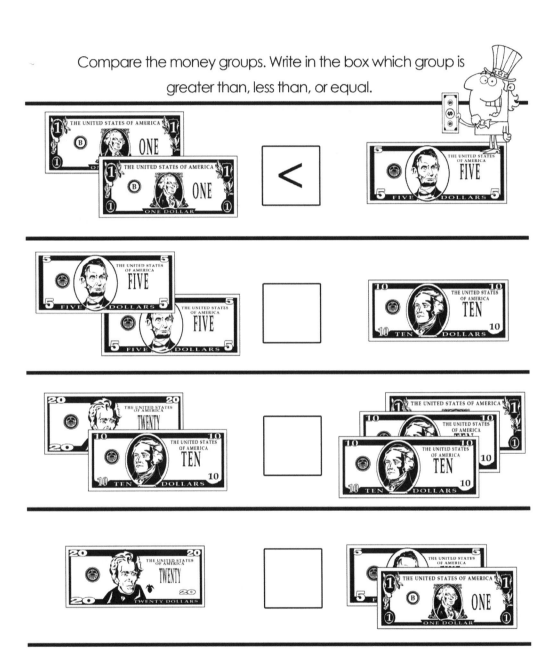

Lesson 6

Dollars - Matching

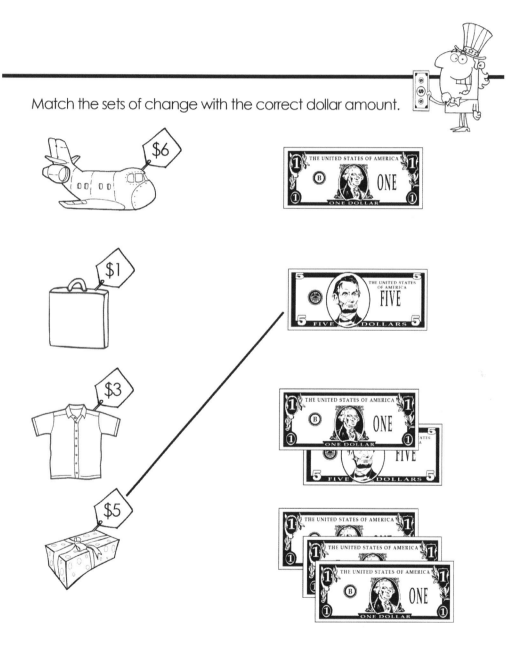

Match the sets of change with the correct dollar amount.

Lesson 7

Counting Dollars and Change 1

Write the total amount of money in the blank.

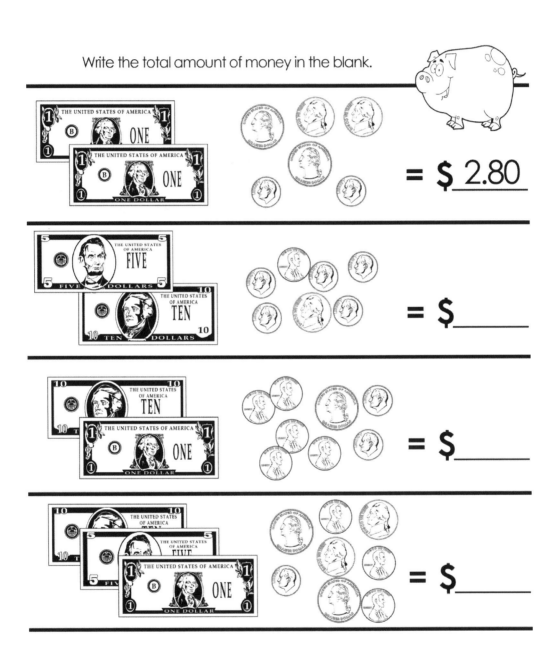

= $ 2.80

= $ _____

= $ _____

= $ _____

Lesson 8

Counting Dollars and Change 2

Write the total amount of money in the blank.

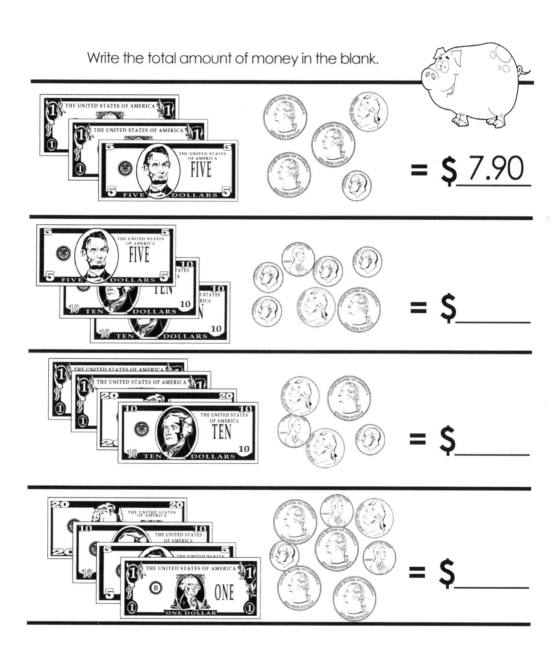

= $ 7.90

= $_____

= $_____

= $_____

Clocks

The hands of the clock tell us what time it is.

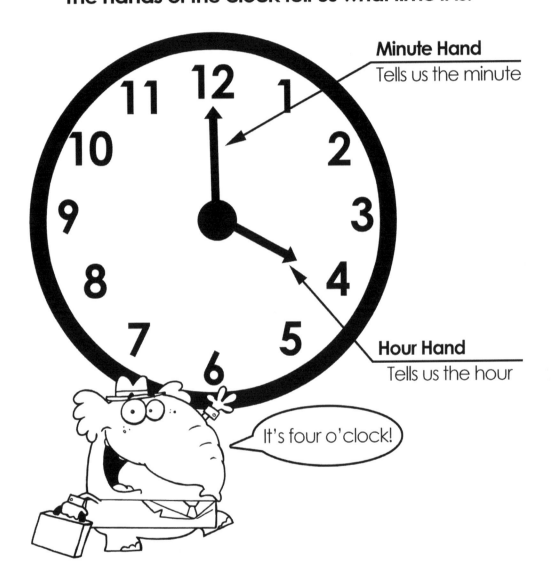

Minute Hand
Tells us the minute

Hour Hand
Tells us the hour

It's four o'clock!

Lesson 1

Identifying Time to the Hour

What time is it? Write the answer under each clock.

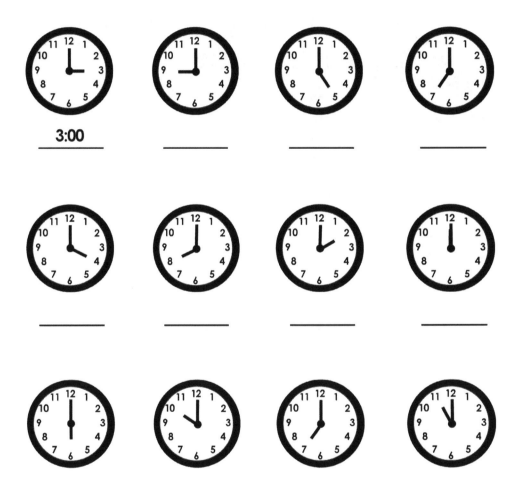

3:00
_____   _____   _____

_____   _____   _____   _____

_____   _____   _____   _____

Identifying Time to the Half- & Quarter-Hour

What time is it? Write the answer under each clock.

3:30
_____

_____

_____

_____

_____

_____

_____

_____

_____

_____

_____

_____

Lesson 2

Writing Time to the Hour

Write the correct time in the clock on the right.

Writing Time 2

Write the correct time in the clock on the right.

Lesson 3

Drawing Time to the Hour

Draw the correct time in the clock on the right.

Drawing Time 2

Draw the correct time in the clock on the right.

Lesson 4

Time Matching

Draw a line from each clock on the left to match
the clock on the right.

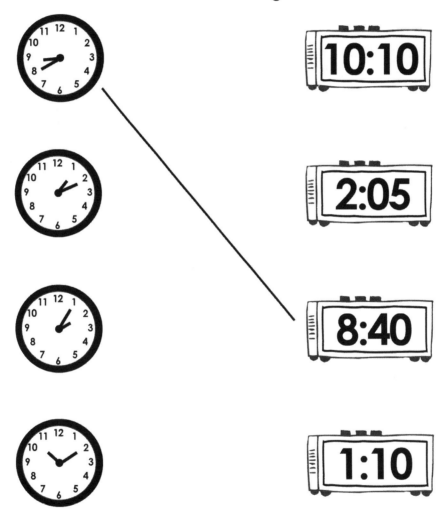

Time Matching 2

Draw a line from each clock on the left to match
the clock on the right.

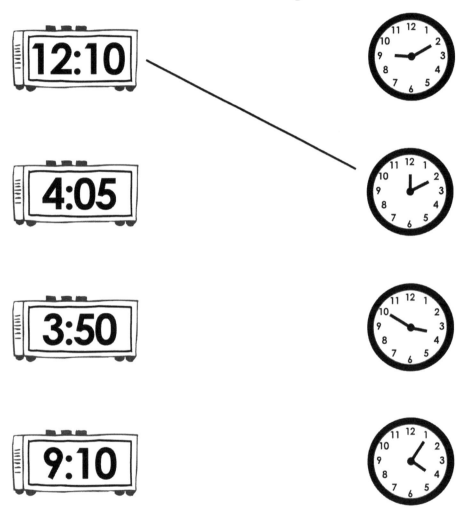

Lesson 5

Time Passage: Hours

Draw the hands on the clock to show the proper times.

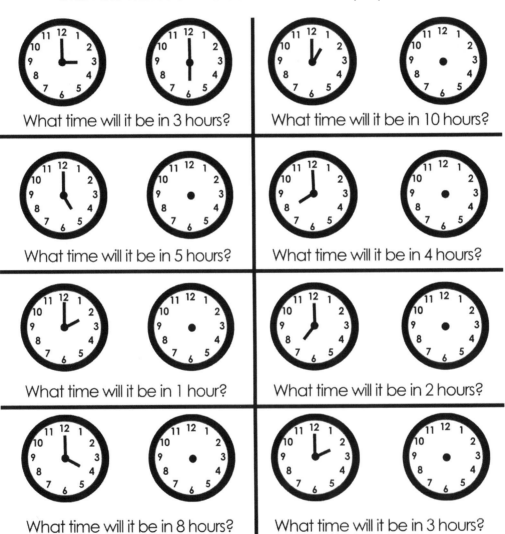

What time will it be in 3 hours?   What time will it be in 10 hours?

What time will it be in 5 hours?   What time will it be in 4 hours?

What time will it be in 1 hour?   What time will it be in 2 hours?

What time will it be in 8 hours?   What time will it be in 3 hours?

Time passage: Half-Hours

Draw the hands on the clock to show the proper times.

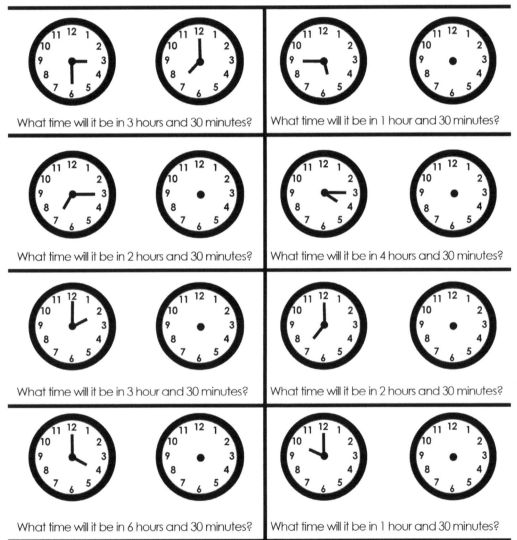

What time will it be in 3 hours and 30 minutes?

What time will it be in 1 hour and 30 minutes?

What time will it be in 2 hours and 30 minutes?

What time will it be in 4 hours and 30 minutes?

What time will it be in 3 hour and 30 minutes?

What time will it be in 2 hours and 30 minutes?

What time will it be in 6 hours and 30 minutes?

What time will it be in 1 hour and 30 minutes?

Time passage: Quarter-Hours

Draw the hands on the clock to show the proper times.

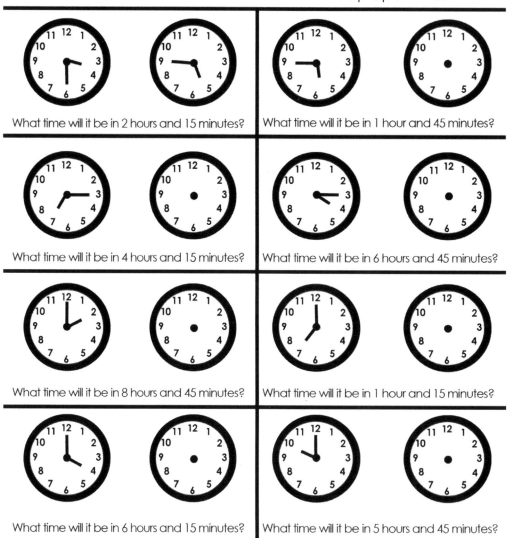

What time will it be in 2 hours and 15 minutes?

What time will it be in 1 hour and 45 minutes?

What time will it be in 4 hours and 15 minutes?

What time will it be in 6 hours and 45 minutes?

What time will it be in 8 hours and 45 minutes?

What time will it be in 1 hour and 15 minutes?

What time will it be in 6 hours and 15 minutes?

What time will it be in 5 hours and 45 minutes?

Lesson 6

Writing Time Passage: Half-Hours

Write the correct times in the clocks on the right.

What time will it be in 3 hours and 30 minutes?

What time will it be in 6 hours and 30 minutes?

What time will it be in 1 hour and 45 minutes?

What time will it be in 3 hours and 30 minutes?

What time will it be in 3 hours and 45 minutes?

What time will it be in 2 hours and 30 minutes?

What time will it be in 9 hours and 15 minutes?

What time will it be in 1 hour and 30 minutes?

Lesson 3

Identifying Liquid Measurements 1

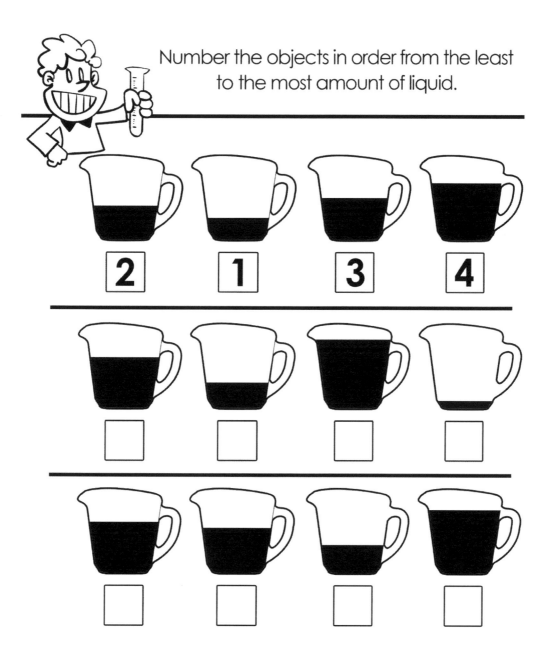

Number the objects in order from the least to the most amount of liquid.

Identifying Liquid Measurements 2

Number the objects in order from the most to the least amount of liquid.

Lesson 4

Identifying Liquid Measurements 3

4 cups = 1 quart

Circle the set that holds more liquid

Lesson 5

Identifying Warmer Temperatures

Circle the warmer temperature.

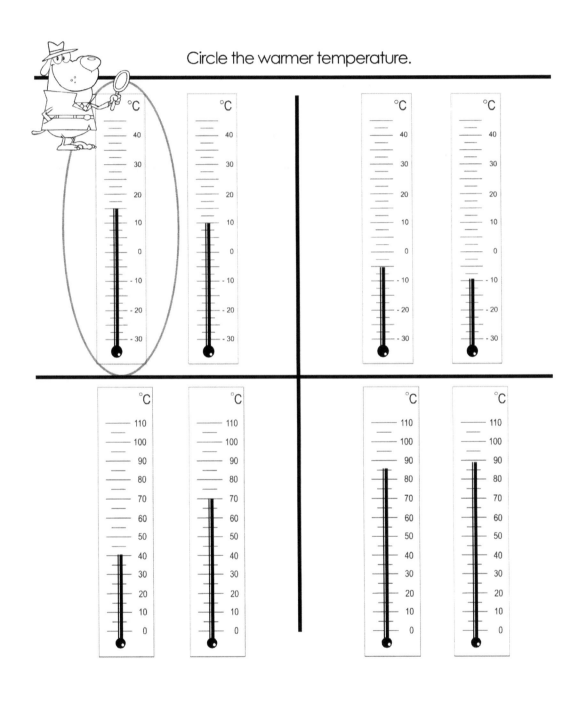

Lesson 6

Identifying Cooler Temperatures

Circle the cooler temperature.

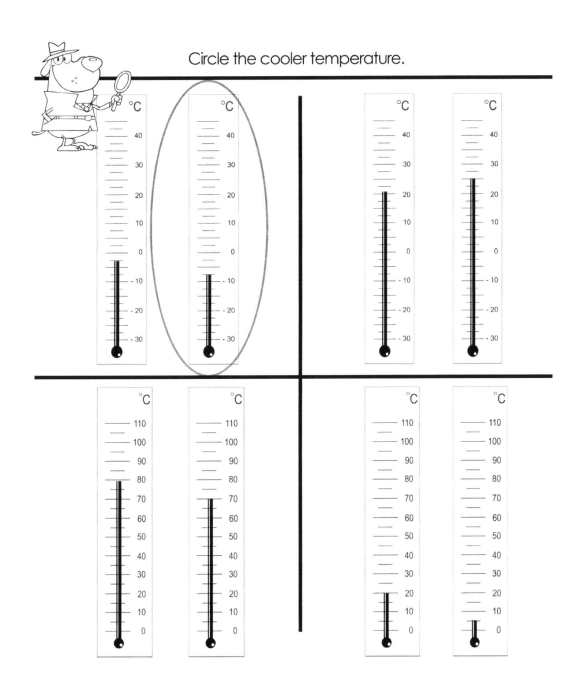

Lesson 7

Drawing Temperatures 1

Draw a line on each thermometer to show the correct temperature.

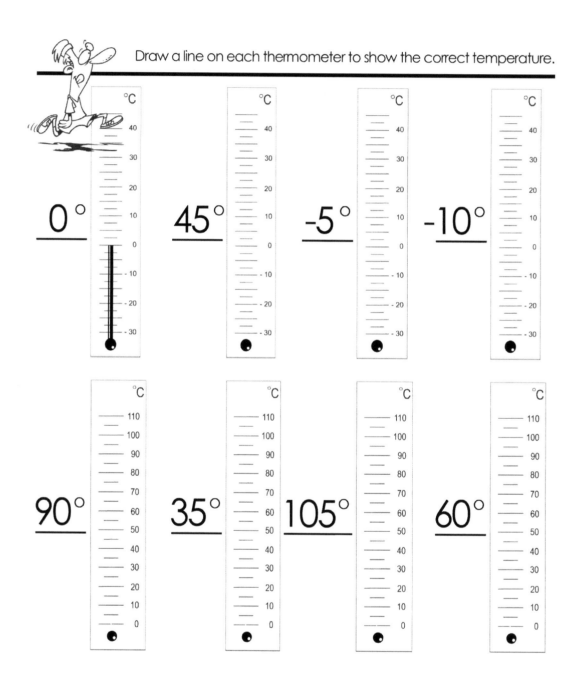

Drawing Temperatures 2

Draw a line on each thermometer to show the correct temperature.

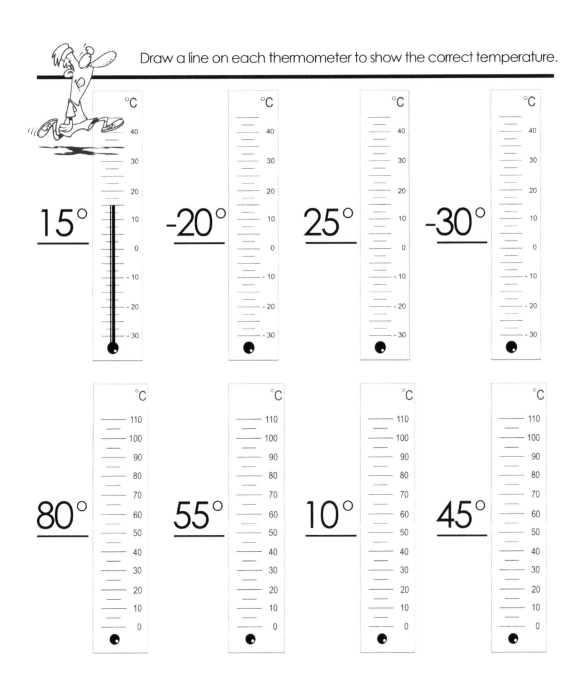

Lesson 8

Writing Temperature

Write the correct temperature in the blank.

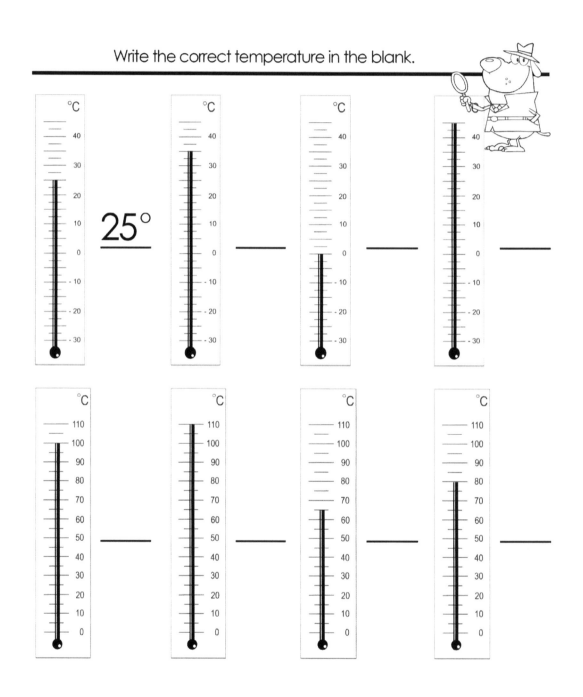

$25°$

Lesson 9

Identifying Length

Number the plants in order from shortest to longest.

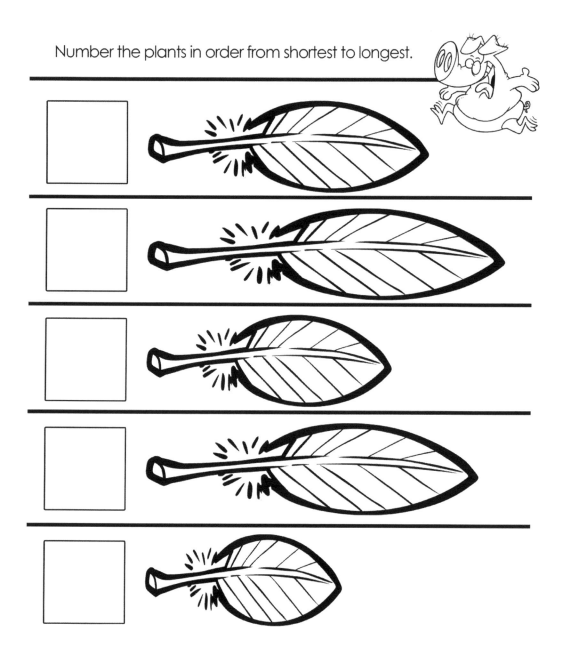

Lesson 10

Identifying Length in Centimeters 1

Write the length of each object in the blank

16 centimeters

_____ centimeters

_____ centimeters

_____ centimeters

_____ centimeters

Identifying Length in Centimeters 2

Write the length of each object in the blank

15 centimeters

_____ centimeters

_____ centimeters

_____ centimeters

_____ centimeters

Identifying Length in Centimeters 3

Write the height of each object in the box

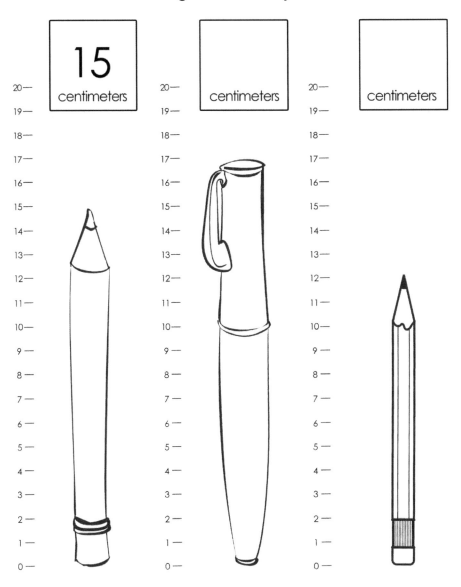

Flat Shapes

Shapes can come in any size and can have many sides. Here are the flat shapes you will need to know for this chapter.

Circle

Triangle

Rectangle

Square

Pentagon

Hexagon

Heptagon

Octagon

Nonagon

Decagon

Solid Shapes

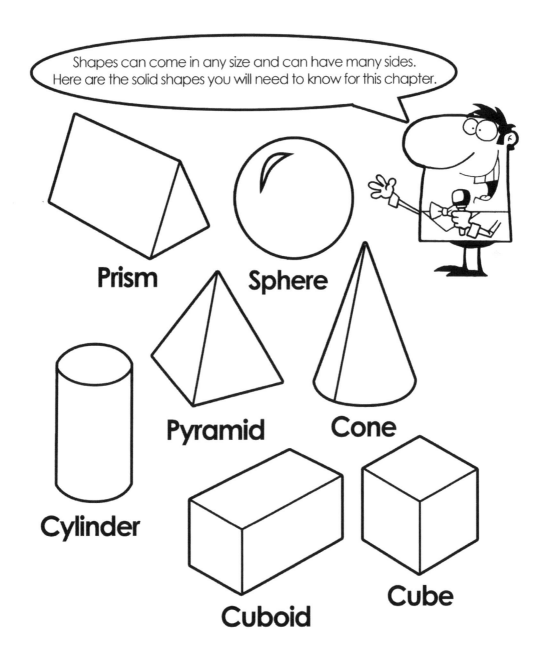

Shapes can come in any size and can have many sides. Here are the solid shapes you will need to know for this chapter.

Prism

Sphere

Pyramid

Cone

Cylinder

Cuboid

Cube

Lesson 1

Identifying Flat Shapes

Write the name of each shape.

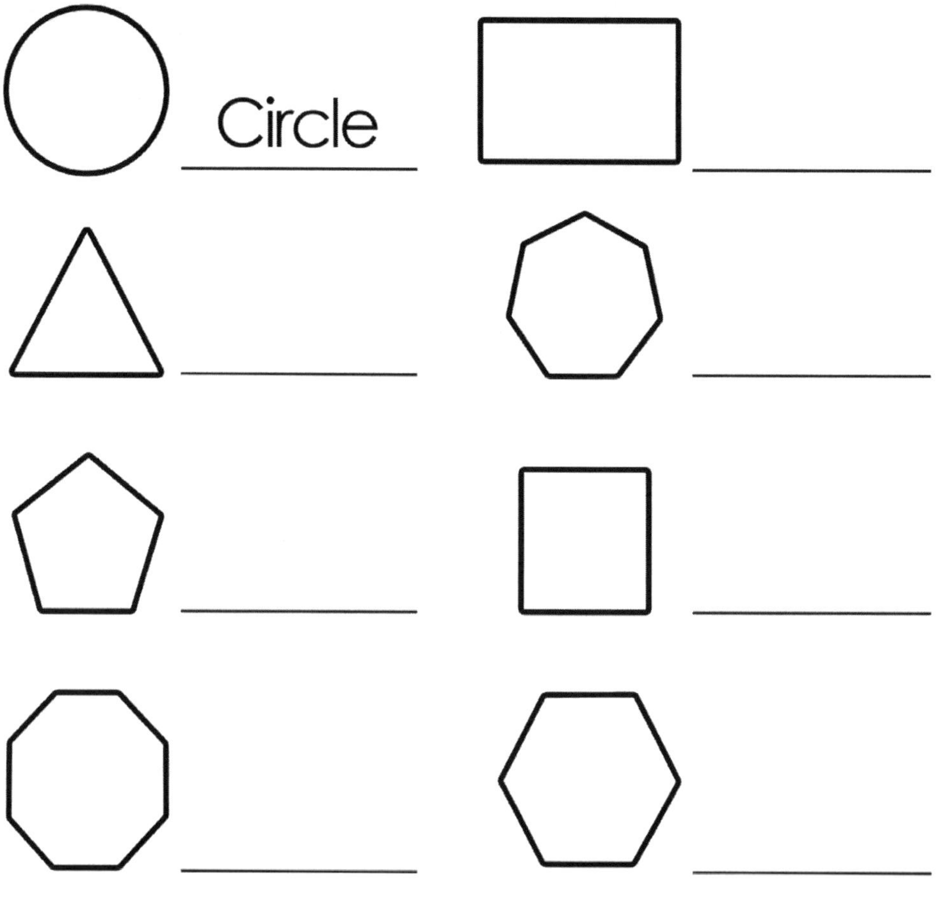

Circle _____

_____

_____

_____

_____

_____

_____

_____

Lesson 2

Identifying Solid Shapes

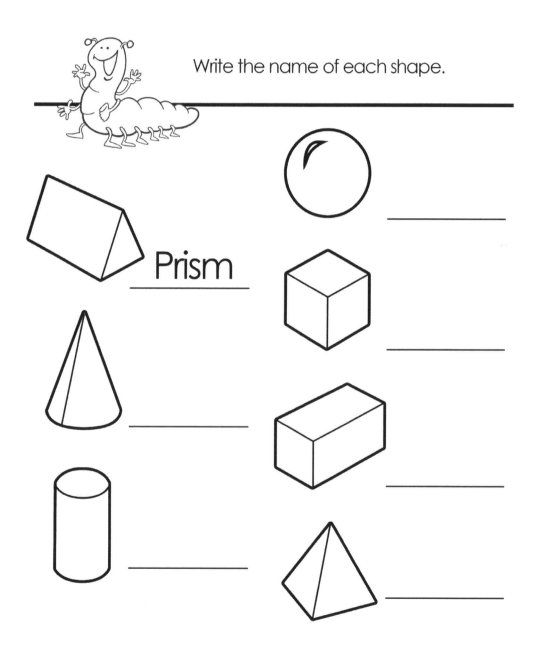

Write the name of each shape.

Prism _____

_____

_____

_____

_____

_____

_____

Lesson 3

Making New Shapes

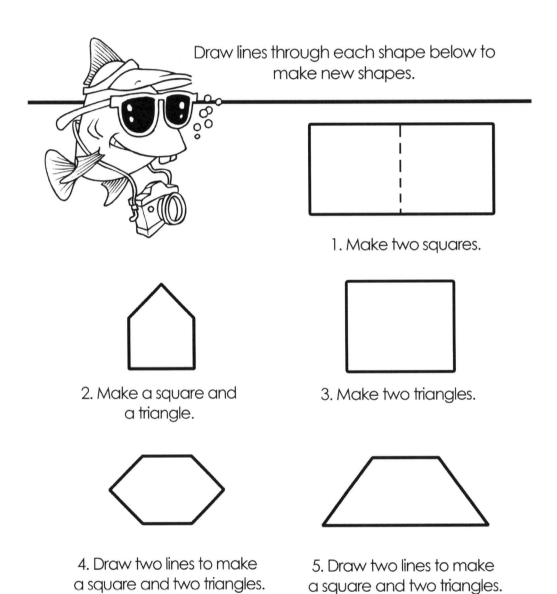

Draw lines through each shape below to make new shapes.

1. Make two squares.

2. Make a square and a triangle.

3. Make two triangles.

4. Draw two lines to make a square and two triangles.

5. Draw two lines to make a square and two triangles.

Lesson 4

Identifying Flat Shapes by Number of Sides

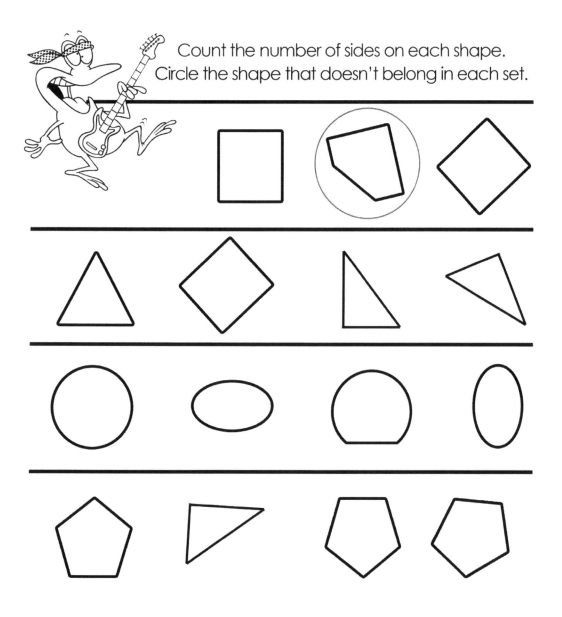

Count the number of sides on each shape.
Circle the shape that doesn't belong in each set.

Lesson 5

Counting Shapes' Sides

Count the sides. Write the answers in the boxes.

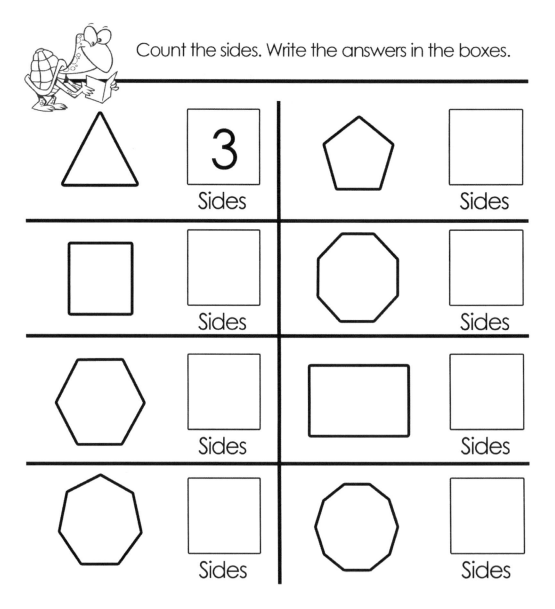

Lesson 6

Comparing Solid Shapes

Circle the objects that are the same as the solid shapes in each row.

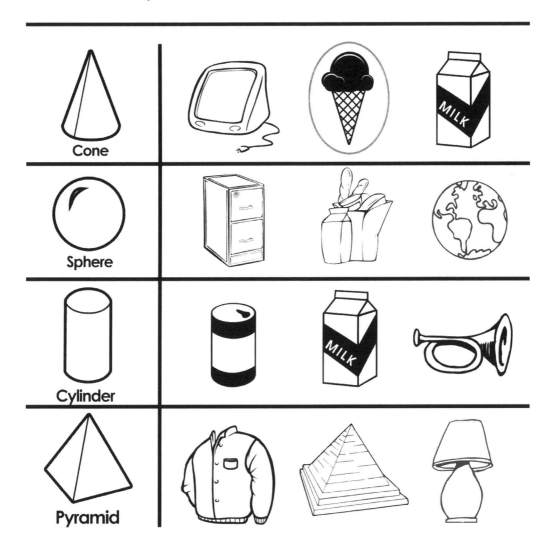

Lesson 7

Symmetry 1

Symmetry is when both halves are the same.
Finish drawing the other side of each shape
to make both sides the same.

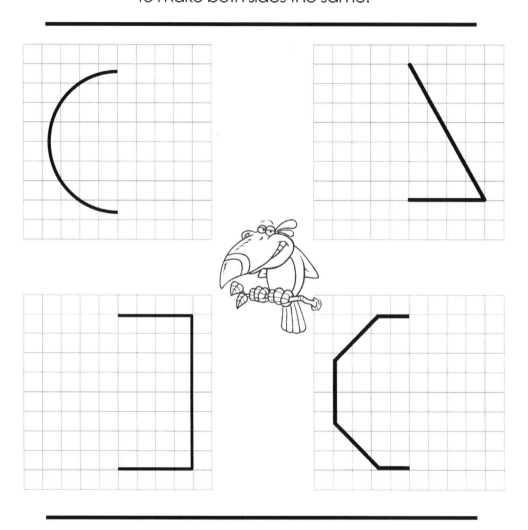

Symmetry 2

Symmetry is when both halves are the same.
Finish drawing the other side of each shape
to make both sides the same.

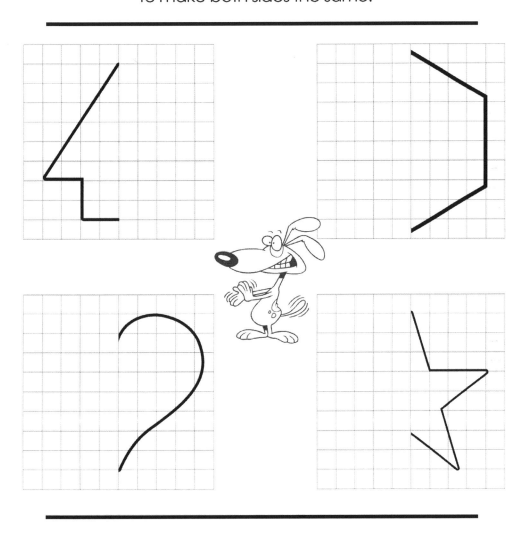

Lesson 8

Creating Multiple Shapes 1

Draw lines through the circles to create the number of parts listed below.

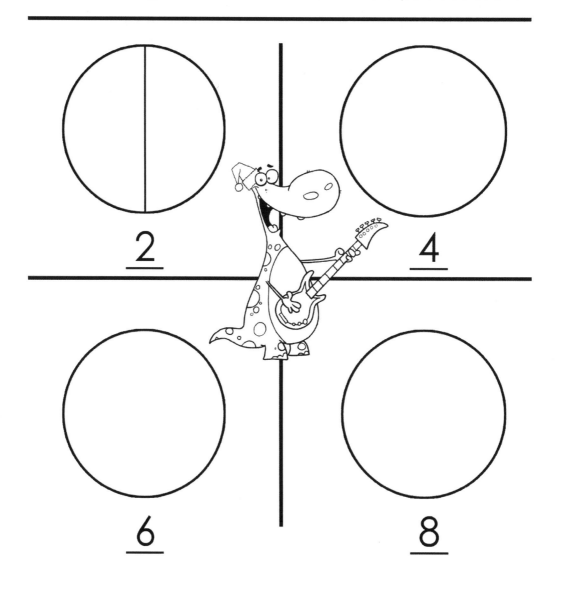

2

4

6

8

Creating Multiple Shapes 2

How many small triangles are in these objects?

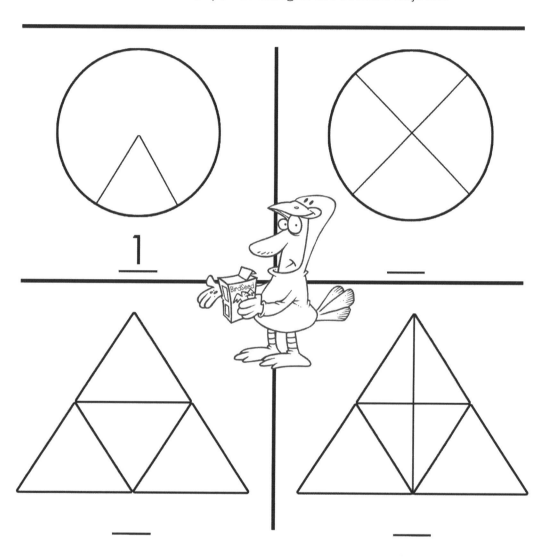

$\underline{\hspace{0.5em}1\hspace{0.5em}}$

$\underline{\hspace{2em}}$

$\underline{\hspace{2em}}$

$\underline{\hspace{2em}}$

Creating Multiple Shapes 3

Draw lines through the squares to cut them in equal parts.

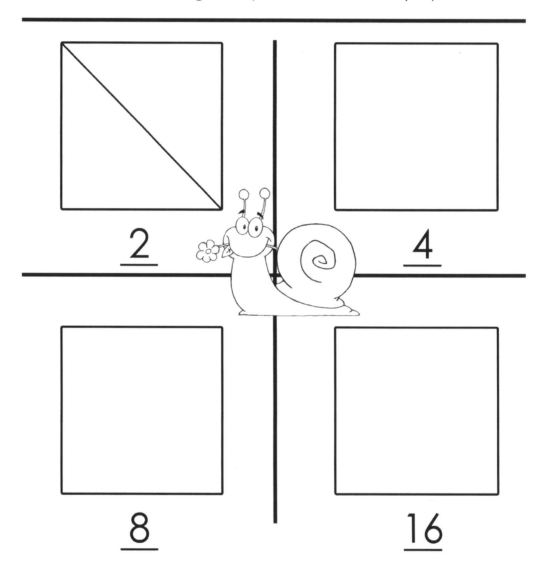

2

4

8

16

Practice Test #1

Practice Questions

1. Sarah had 80 cupcakes to sell at a bake sale. She sold 70 cupcakes. Then Sarah's mom brought 20 more cupcakes for Sarah to sell at the bake sale. Which expression can be used to find out how many cupcakes, c, Sarah now has?

   Ⓐ $80 - 70 + 20 = c$

   Ⓑ $80 + 70 - 20 = c$

   Ⓒ $80 - 70 - 20 = c$

   Ⓓ $80 + 70 + 20 = c$

2. Last week, Lucas had 55 marbles. He lost some marbles when he dropped his marble bag outside. Now Lucas has 32 marbles. Which equation can be used to show the amount of marbles, m, that Lucas lost?

   Ⓐ $55 - m = 32$

   Ⓑ $m - 55 = 32$

   Ⓒ $m - 32 = 55$

   Ⓓ $m + 32 = 55$

3. What is the sum of 7 and 6?

   Ⓐ 11

   Ⓑ 12

   Ⓒ 13

   Ⓓ 14

4. What is the sum of 9 and 5?

Ⓐ 11

Ⓑ 12

Ⓒ 13

Ⓓ 14

5. Which pair of equal numbers add to 16?

Ⓐ 7 + 7

Ⓑ 8 + 8

Ⓒ 9 + 9

Ⓓ 10+10

6. Which equation can be used to determine the number of squares to the right?

Ⓐ $4 + 4 + 4 + 4 = 16$

Ⓑ $5 + 5 + 5 + 5 = 20$

Ⓒ $6 + 6 + 6 + 6 = 24$

Ⓓ $7 + 7 + 7 + 7 = 28$

7. 8 hundreds, 5 tens, and 3 ones is equivalent to which number?

Ⓐ 853

Ⓑ 835

Ⓒ 583

Ⓓ 538

8. Ten tens is the same as which number?

Ⓐ one

Ⓑ ten

Ⓒ one thousand

Ⓓ one hundred

9. Bosco started counting to 1000. He said "5, 10, 15, 20, ..." Was Bosco counting by 5s, 10s, 100s, or 1000s?

Ⓐ 5s

Ⓑ 10s

Ⓒ 100s

Ⓓ 1000s

10. How is the number 645 read in expanded form?

Ⓐ six hundred fifty-four

Ⓑ six hundred forty-five

Ⓒ six thousand forty-five

Ⓓ six thousand four hundred fifty

11. Which symbol can be used to complete the statement: 367 _____ 376?

Ⓐ =

Ⓑ >

Ⓒ <

Ⓓ Cannot be determined

12. Which symbol can be used to complete the statement: 538 ____438?

Ⓐ =

Ⓑ >

Ⓒ <

Ⓓ Cannot be determined

13. Determine the sum of 54 and 27.

Ⓐ 71

Ⓑ 73

Ⓒ 81

Ⓓ 83

14. Determine the difference of 71 and 34.

Ⓐ 43

Ⓑ 34

Ⓒ 47

Ⓓ 37

15. Add $41 + 23 + 57$.

Ⓐ 121

Ⓑ 1211

Ⓒ 111

Ⓓ 1111

16. Add $36 + 51 + 29 + 4$.

Ⓐ 1020

Ⓑ 120

Ⓒ 156

Ⓓ 1416

17. Subtract $786 - 452$.

Ⓐ 443

Ⓑ 338

Ⓒ 344

Ⓓ 334

18. Subtract $800 - 10$.

   Ⓐ 810

   Ⓑ 710

   Ⓒ 890

   Ⓓ 790

19. Add $543 + 100$

   Ⓐ 553

   Ⓑ 544

   Ⓒ 1543

   Ⓓ 643

20. Julius used number blocks to determine the sum of 213 and 145. Using the blocks that Julius created, what is $213 + 145$?

   Ⓐ 358

   Ⓑ 258

   Ⓒ 355

   Ⓓ 345

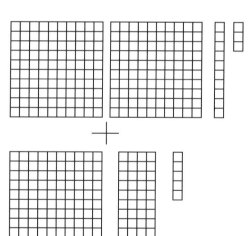

21. Use a ruler to measure the distance of the line segment in inches.

   Ⓐ 1 inch

   Ⓑ 2 inches

   Ⓒ 3 inches

   Ⓓ 4 inches

22. Use a ruler to measure the distance of the line segment in both inches and centimeters. Round your answer to the nearest whole unit.

Ⓐ 3 inches, 5 centimeters

Ⓑ 2 inches, 5 centimeters

—————————

Ⓒ 2 inches, 6 centimeters

Ⓓ 2 inches, 4 centimeters

23. Which length is the best estimate for the thickness of an encyclopedia?

Ⓐ 2 inches

Ⓑ 2 feet

Ⓒ 2 yards

Ⓓ 2 meters

24. How much longer is line segment AB than line segment CD? Round your answer to the nearest centimeter.

Ⓐ 2 centimeters

Ⓑ 4 centimeters

A ——————————— B

Ⓒ 6 centimeters

C ———————— D

Ⓓ 7 centimeters

25. Rebecca was 57 meters away from her home and walked 32 meters towards her home. Which equation represents the number of meters Rebecca is away from her home now?

Ⓐ 57 meters + 32 meters = 89 meters

Ⓑ 57 meters - 32 meters = 25 meters

Ⓒ 57 meters - 32 meters = 35 meters

Ⓓ 57 meters + 32 meters = 99 meters

26. How much longer is line segment EF than line segment GH?

Ⓐ 4 units

Ⓑ 16 units

Ⓒ 10 units

Ⓓ 12 units

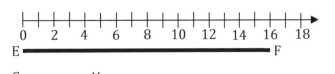

27. What time does the clock read?

Ⓐ 10:04

Ⓑ 10:40

Ⓒ 4:50

Ⓓ 10:20

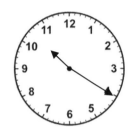

28. If you have 3 dollar bills, 3 quarters, 1 dime, 1 nickel, and 3 pennies, how much money do you have?

Ⓐ $3.93

Ⓑ $3.98

Ⓒ $4.03

Ⓓ $4.08

29. Which collection of money below can be used to represent $2.42?

Ⓐ 2 dollar bills, 3 dimes, 2 nickels, and 2 pennies

Ⓑ 2 dollar bills, 2 quarters, and 2 pennies

Ⓒ 2 dollar bills, 1 quarter, 1 dime, and 2 pennies

Ⓓ 2 dollar bills, 3 quarters, 2 dimes and 2 pennies?

30. Which line plot can be used to represent a length of 12 units?

Ⓐ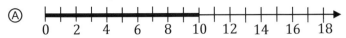

Ⓑ

Ⓒ

Ⓓ

Use the following bar graph to answer the questions 31 and 32:

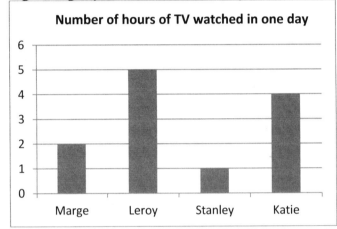

31. How many more hours of TV did Leroy watch than Marge?

Ⓐ 2 hours

Ⓑ 5 hours

Ⓒ 3 hours

Ⓓ 4 hours

32. What is the total number of hours Stanley and Katie watched together on that day?

Ⓐ 5 hours

Ⓑ 4 hours

Ⓒ 3 hours

Ⓓ 1 hour

33. What is a name of the shape at the right?

Ⓐ triangle

Ⓑ quadrilateral

Ⓒ pentagon

Ⓓ hexagon

34. Identify the shape at the right.

Ⓐ triangle

Ⓑ quadrilateral

Ⓒ pentagon

Ⓓ hexagon

35. The rectangle at the right has been divided into 3 rows and 4 columns of same-size squares. How many total squares make up the rectangle?

Ⓐ 10 squares

Ⓑ 12 squares

Ⓒ 14 squares

Ⓓ 16 squares

36. What part of the circle is shaded?

Ⓐ a half

Ⓑ a third

Ⓒ a fourth

Ⓓ Cannot be determined

Practice Test #2

Practice Questions

1. Jackie was 56 miles away from her home. She then drove 32 miles towards her home, turned around and traveled 12 miles away from her home to stay at a friend's house. Which equation can be used to determine the number of miles, m, that Jackie is away from her home while she is at her friend's house?

   Ⓐ $56 + 32 - 12 = m$

   Ⓑ $56 - 32 + 12 = m$

   Ⓒ $56 + 32 + 12 = m$

   Ⓓ $56 - 32 - 12 = m$

2. Horace had an unknown number of student handbooks he was passing out at the beginning of a school day. He passed out 85 handbooks and had 12 handbooks remaining at the end of the day. Which equation can be used to determine the number of handbooks, h, that Horace had at the beginning of the school day?

   Ⓐ $85 - h = 12$

   Ⓑ $h - 85 = 12$

   Ⓒ $85 - 12 = h$

   Ⓓ $h + 12 = 85$

3. Subtract $18 - 7$.

   Ⓐ 11

   Ⓑ 10

   Ⓒ 9

   Ⓓ 8

4. Add $8 + 11$.

    Ⓐ 16

    Ⓑ 17

    Ⓒ 18

    Ⓓ 19

5. Determine if Groups 1 and 2 have an odd or even number of squares.

    Ⓐ Group 1: even; Group 2: even

    Ⓑ Group 1: odd; Group 2: even

    Ⓒ Group 1: even; Group 2: odd

    Ⓓ Group 1: odd; Group 2: odd

6. Which expression represents how to determine the number of circles there are in the set below.

    Ⓐ $3 + 3 + 3$

    Ⓑ $4 + 4 + 4 + 4$

    Ⓒ $2 + 2$

    Ⓓ $2 + 2 + 2 + 2$

7. 403 is the equal to which expression?

    Ⓐ 4 hundreds, 0 tens, and 3 ones

    Ⓑ 4 hundreds, 3 tens, and 0 ones

    Ⓒ 4 thousands and 3 ones

    Ⓓ 4 hundreds, 3 tens, and 3 ones

8. 2 hundreds, 5 tens, and 6 ones is equal to which number?

    Ⓐ 265   Ⓒ 256

    Ⓑ 652   Ⓓ 625

9. What are the first five terms when counting to 1000 by 100s?

Ⓐ 1, 2, 3, 4, 5

Ⓑ 5, 10, 15, 20, 25

Ⓒ 100, 200, 300, 400, 500

Ⓓ 3, 6, 9, 12, 15

10. How is the number 367 written in expanded form?

Ⓐ Three hundred sixty-seven

Ⓑ Three thousand six hundred seven

Ⓒ Three hundred seventy-six

Ⓓ Three hundred sixteen-seven

11. Which symbol is used to complete the statement: 279_____311?

Ⓐ =

Ⓑ >

Ⓒ <

Ⓓ Cannot be determined

12. Which symbol is used to complete the statement: 516_____516?

Ⓐ =

Ⓑ >

Ⓒ <

Ⓓ Cannot be determined

13. Add $23 + 45.$

   Ⓐ 86

   Ⓑ 59

   Ⓒ 75

   Ⓓ 68

14. Subtract $43 - 26.$

   Ⓐ 15

   Ⓑ 16

   Ⓒ 17

   Ⓓ 23

15. Add $24 + 47 + 51 + 13.$

   Ⓐ 125

   Ⓑ 1215

   Ⓒ 135

   Ⓓ 1315

16. Add $17 + 77 + 25 + 95.$

   Ⓐ 214

   Ⓑ 2024

   Ⓒ 204

   Ⓓ 224

17. Add $455 + 618.$

   Ⓐ 1073

   Ⓑ 1063

   Ⓒ 1163

   Ⓓ 1083

18. Subtract $841 - 153$.

Ⓐ 688

Ⓑ 712

Ⓒ 692

Ⓓ 678

19. Subtract $743 - 10$.

Ⓐ 643

Ⓑ 733

Ⓒ 742

Ⓓ 753

20. Sandra wants to simplify $587 - 126$. **What is the first step Sandra should take to subtract the two numbers?**

Ⓐ Add the 1 and the 5.

Ⓑ Subtract the 6 from the 7.

Ⓒ Subtract the 2 from the 8.

Ⓓ Add the 6 and 7.

21. Use a ruler to measure the length of the line segment in centimeters.

Ⓐ 6 centimeters

Ⓑ 7 centimeters

Ⓒ 8 centimeters

Ⓓ 9 centimeters

22. Use a ruler to measure the length of the line segment in inches and centimeters. Round your answer to the nearest whole unit.

——————————————————

 Ⓐ 4 inches; 9 centimeters

 Ⓑ 4 inches; 10 centimeters

 Ⓒ 3 inches; 9 centimeters

 Ⓓ 3 inches; 10 centimeters

23. Which length is the best estimate for the height of a dinner table?

 Ⓐ 1 inch

 Ⓑ 1 foot

 Ⓒ 1 yard

 Ⓓ 1 mile

24. The first arrow is how many centimeters longer than the second arrow?

 Ⓐ 1 centimeter

 Ⓑ 2 centimeters

 Ⓒ 3 centimeters

 Ⓓ 4 centimeters

25. The sides of a triangle are 13 centimeters, 18 centimeters, and 21 centimeters. What is the total distance around the triangle?

 Ⓐ 52 centimeters

 Ⓑ 53 centimeters

 Ⓒ 54 centimeters

 Ⓓ 412 centimeters

26. Use the given number line given to find the sum of 8 and 6.

Ⓐ 14

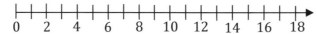

Ⓑ 8

Ⓒ 2

Ⓓ 16

27. What time does the clock read?

Ⓐ 10:40

Ⓑ 8: 02

Ⓒ 8:10

Ⓓ 9:10

28. If you have 1 dollar bill, 2 quarters, 4 dimes, 1 nickel, and 1 penny, how much money do you have?

Ⓐ $1.91

Ⓑ $1.96

Ⓒ $2.01

Ⓓ $1.92

29. Which collection of money can be used to represent $0.94?

Ⓐ 3 quarters, 1 nickel, 4 pennies

Ⓑ 3 quarters, 1 dime, 1 nickel, 4 pennies

Ⓒ 9 nickels, 4 pennies

Ⓓ 4 quarters, 6 pennies

30. Which line plot can be used to represent a length of 8 units?

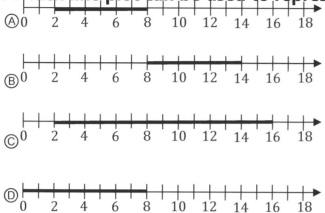

Use the bar graph below to answer problems #31 and #32.

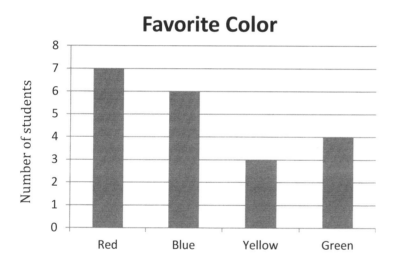

31. How many students were asked their favorite color for this chart?

Ⓐ 16

Ⓑ 20

Ⓒ 18

Ⓓ 22

32. How many more students chose red as their favorite color than those who chose yellow as their favorite color?

Ⓐ 3

Ⓑ 4

Ⓒ 5

Ⓓ 6

33. What shape has exactly 3 angles and 3 sides?

Ⓐ Triangle

Ⓑ Quadrilateral

Ⓒ Pentagon

Ⓓ Hexagon

34. What shape has exactly 4 angles?

Ⓐ Triangle

Ⓑ Quadrilateral

Ⓒ Pentagon

Ⓓ Hexagon

35. A rectangle has been divided so it has five columns and four rows consisting of same-size squares, as shown in the figure below. How many same-size squares are there?

Ⓐ 15

Ⓑ 18

Ⓒ 19

Ⓓ 20

36. The rectangle has been divided into equal shares. What share is represented by the shading?

Ⓐ One-half

Ⓑ One-third

Ⓒ One-fourth

Ⓓ One whole

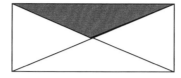

Thank You

We at Mometrix would like to extend our heartfelt thanks to you, our friend and patron, for allowing us to play a part in your journey. It is a privilege to serve people from all walks of life who are unified in their commitment to building the best future they can for themselves.

The preparation you devote to these important testing milestones may be the most valuable educational opportunity you have for making a real difference in your life. We encourage you to put your heart into it—that feeling of succeeding, overcoming, and yes, conquering will be well worth the hours you've invested.

We want to hear your story, your struggles and your successes, and if you see any opportunities for us to improve our materials so we can help others even more effectively in the future, please share that with us as well. **The team at Mometrix would be absolutely thrilled to hear from you!** So please, send us an email (support@mometrix.com) and let's stay in touch.

Additional Bonus Material

Due to our efforts to try to keep this book to a manageable length, we've created a link that will give you access to all of your additional bonus material.

Please visit http://www.mometrix.com/bonus948/terrag2math to access the information.